D1793255

Geography of the United States

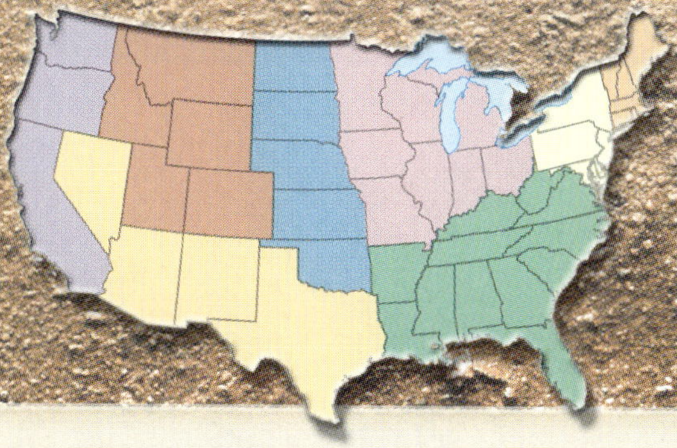

Contents

1 The United States

Exploring the United States of America The United States stretches about 3,000 miles from coast to coast. Because of its great size, it is often divided into smaller geographical areas, or regions. The states in each region share many things, such as geography, climate, and natural resources.

Regions of the United States

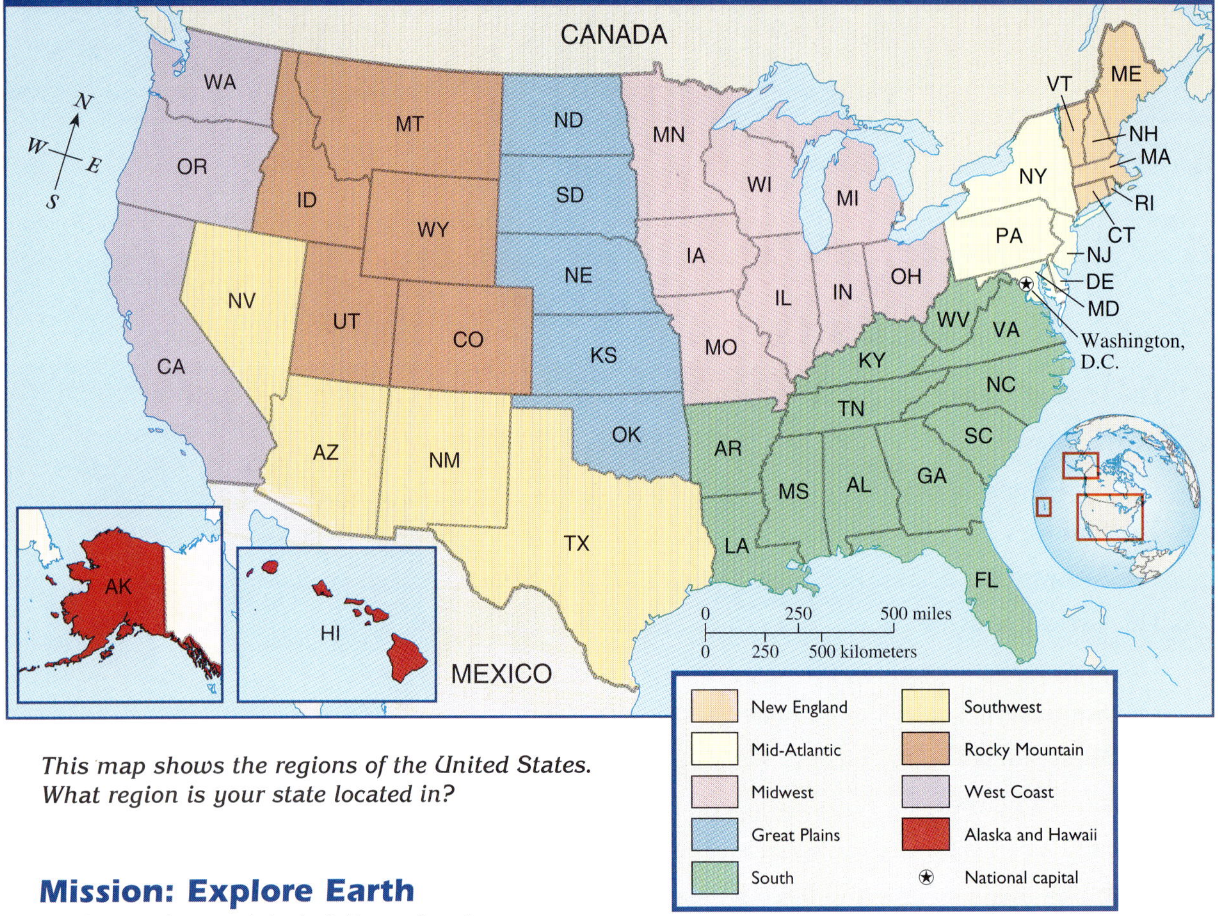

This map shows the regions of the United States. What region is your state located in?

Mission: Explore Earth

As you know, Admiral Zorg, for almost a year the spaceship that I command has been exploring the planet known as Earth. Exploring Earth has been fun and exciting. We have discovered it to be very different from our planet Proteus. We have observed its interesting physical features and life forms and reported our observations to you. Now our year of exploring draws to a close. There is one last place we have to see and describe—the United States of America.

After we explore each area of the country we will send you a report. In each report, we will answer questions, such as: Which states make up each **region**? What does the land look like in this region? What

> **vocabulary**
> **region** an area of land whose parts have one or more common characteristics

sort of plants and animals live there? What is the weather like? How do the people make their livings? What do they eat and drink? How do they enjoy themselves?

We decided that we would send you a report from each region of the United States. These are the regions we will report from: New England; the Mid-Atlantic; the South; the Midwest; the Great Plains; the Rocky Mountains; the Southwest; and the West Coast. There are also two states which don't belong to a region, because they are not connected to any other state. They are called Alaska and Hawaii. We will send a separate report from these two states.

We will gather information for our reports by looking at things. When we have questions we will talk to some of the people we meet. (Of course, we will always remember to be disguised as human beings!)

Right now, as I record this audio message, we are flying over a huge body of water called the Atlantic Ocean. The next land we see will be the United States of America.

A Vast and Varied Country

The United States of America is reported to be a huge country. Earthlings in other places have described it as having a great variety of **landforms** and life forms. I have heard, too, that it is full of many different kinds of people. This is because people have traveled from all over the world to live there.

vocabulary
landform a feature of the earth's surface created by nature

Before we left the last country we visited, we remembered to buy some maps of the United States. These will help us find the places we want to go. They will also help us to identify the different areas of this vast country.

You remember, Admiral, that Earth is shaped like a globe, or sphere. Earthlings divide their world into two half-globes, or hemispheres. They speak of an Eastern Hemisphere and a Western Hemisphere.

The United States is in the Western Hemisphere, on the continent called North America. A continent is a big landmass that sometimes has islands off its shores. On the mainland of North America, the northernmost country is called Canada. The southernmost country is called Mexico. And, in the middle of the continent, there is the United States of America.

Looking at our maps, we see that the United States stretches all the way across the continent of North America—a distance of about 3,000 miles. On each side of the country, there is a huge body of water called an ocean. On the west side, the United States borders on the Pacific Ocean. On the east side, it borders on the Atlantic Ocean.

Lieutenant Koola just informed me that she's sighted land below us. She's pretty sure that it is the state of Maine, in the northeastern United States. Our map shows that the country is divided into 50 smaller units, or states. I bet that's why they call it the United States!

Each of the 50 states has its own government and its own capital city. This is because the United States is a democracy. In other words, it has a system of government in which the people rule through elected representatives. The head of the national government, or all 50 states, is called the President. He lives in a place called Washington, D.C., which is the capital of the United States.

Now, we are flying low over the coast of Maine. Through the spaceship's porthole I can see huge, gray waves crashing against tall cliffs, which are covered with evergreen trees. We will look for a place where people live and land there. We are all very excited to meet our first Americans. In my next report, I hope to have plenty to tell you about this interesting country.

I've given the order to turn on the invisibility shield and start our descent.

2 New England

Exploring New England **This region is in the northeastern part of the United States. It is made up of six states—Maine, New Hampshire, Vermont, Massachusetts, Connecticut, and Rhode Island. The Atlantic Ocean is a boundary to all of these states except one—Vermont.**

The New England Region

The Appalachian Mountains, a major feature of this region, are among the oldest mountains on Earth.

In my last message, Admiral, I told you how we arrived in the state of Maine. After flying over the coast for a while, we located a town. Lieutenant Koola landed our ship in a forest outside the town. The town had lots of wooden houses and a small harbor with sailboats. The people we met were friendly.

We were hungry because we hadn't eaten since taking off from the other side of the ocean. So we asked someone to tell us where a restaurant was. As you know, one of the things we like to find out about a place is what sort of food the people who live there eat.

When we were all seated in a nearby restaurant, we said we wanted to try one of the special foods of the area. The waiter said, "What about some lobster?" Since we had never heard of lobster, we thought we'd give it a try.

Imagine our surprise when the waiter brought each of us what looked like a gigantic red bug! It had long antennae and big mean-looking claws. By talking to the waiter, we figured out that lobsters come from the sea, so they aren't really bugs. We were relieved to hear that!

Lobster traps are piled high on the shore of a Maine town. To the right, a lobsterer removes his catch from a trap.

The waiter mentioned that many people in this part of Maine make their living by catching lobster. We asked him where we could go to find out more about the area. He said, "You could try the public library." We didn't know what a public library was, but we were curious. The waiter gave us directions, and after we left the restaurant we went looking for one.

Learning at the Library

The library turned out to be a brick building on the main street. When we went inside, we realized that we had made a great discovery. A public library, Admiral, is a place full of books that people can come to read without paying anything. Most public libraries also have computers, and between the books and the computers, you can find information on any subject.

In America, there are thousands and thousands of these libraries. Almost every town or city has at least one. As soon as we found this out, we realized that we had a wonderful new way to find information. We decided that every time we came to a new place, we would spend some time in the public library, gathering facts.

Here are some of the things we learned about Maine. You remember, Admiral, that Maine is in the northeastern part of the United States. It is one of six northeastern states that make up the region called New England. The others are New Hampshire, Vermont, Massachusetts, Connecticut, and Rhode Island.

In terms of **climate**, New England has four very different seasons. It has a cool spring, a warm summer, a crisp fall, and a long, cold, snowy winter.

> **vocabulary**
> **climate** the pattern of weather in a place over a long period of time

You may wonder why the area is called New England. It is because in the 1600s, people from the European country called England crossed the Atlantic Ocean and settled in the area. They also settled further south, all the way down the Atlantic coast.

Then, in the late 1700s the English who had settled in America decided they wanted to break away from England, which was now called Great

Britain. They wanted to set up a country of their own. In the year 1776 they declared their independence from Great Britain. The new country was called the United States of America.

The ruler of Great Britain tried to keep the Americans from breaking away. He sent troops to fight the American army. After several years of war, which the Americans call the Revolutionary War, the United States defeated Great Britain. It established itself as an independent country. But the Americans still kept some British ideas and customs. Most important, they kept the English language, which is spoken by almost all Americans today.

Spectators come from all over the world to enjoy the brilliantly colored leaves of autumn in New England.

After a few days of studying in the library, we were anxious to begin exploring again. But we knew that we would miss the little Maine town and its kind people. Even more, we would miss the delicious lobster.

Mountains and Skyscrapers

After taking off, we turned the ship southwest, toward the mountainous states of New Hampshire and Vermont. Flying low over the mountains, we were greeted by a spectacular sight. Because it was Earth's season of autumn, the green leaves of the trees had changed color. Some of the trees were gold, some red, some purple. Every hillside was ablaze with different colors.

As we flew down for a closer look, Lieutenant Koola pointed to some of the most brilliantly colored trees. "Do you see those trees?" she asked. "A book I was reading said that those were sugar maples. A sweet sauce that is called maple syrup is made from the sap of those trees." You really have to hand it to the Americans, Admiral. They seem to be able to make tasty food out of almost anything—even tree sap and big bugs from the ocean!

From Vermont, we flew south, across the western part of the state of Massachusetts, where we enjoyed the sight of more rolling hills and colorful trees. But we were eager to see the city of Boston, which we knew was the capital of Massachusetts as well as the biggest city in New England. So we turned back east, toward the coast.

Boston looks nothing at all like the small town we visited in Maine. It is a huge, bustling city, full of the tall modern buildings that Americans call skyscrapers. But parts of it are very old. In fact, Boston was the first important city in the United States. When we went to the public library to study, we discovered that it was the oldest public library in the United States. We also learned that there is a local university called Harvard, which was the first college founded in America. Today, Boston is famous as a center of education, with dozens of colleges scattered around town.

Boston is also a city full of history. The Revolutionary War broke out in the Boston area. When we walked through the city on the Freedom Trail, we saw many places important in the story of the Revolution.

We visited Faneuil Hall, an old brick building where the revolutionaries gave speeches against the British. We also saw the house of Paul Revere, one of the heroes of the Revolution. When British troops invaded, he rode out in the middle of the night to warn people that they were coming. A famous old poem talks about "the midnight ride of Paul Revere."

We could have spent much more time in Boston, but we knew we had to fly on to explore the region known as the Mid-Atlantic. So we returned to our ship and headed south and west. Right now we're over the two southern states of New England—Rhode Island and Connecticut. We can see from our map that Rhode Island is by far the smallest of the 50 states, less than 50 miles across. Both Connecticut and Rhode Island have **port** towns as well as some larger cities.

vocabulary
port a place on a river, lake, or ocean where ships can safely unload and load supplies

But speaking of cities, Admiral, the crew is getting excited because our next stop is the biggest city in the whole United States—New York, New York.

Villagers awake to the sound of Paul Revere's midnight call in this painting, "Midnight Ride of Paul Revere" by the American artist, Grant Wood.

© Estate of Grant Wood/Licensed by VAGA, New York, NY

3 The Mid-Atlantic Region

Exploring the Mid-Atlantic Region **This region is located near the middle of the Atlantic coastline. It includes five states—New York, New Jersey, Pennsylvania, Delaware, Maryland—and the city of Washington, D.C., the capital of the United States.**

There are many port cities in the Mid-Atlantic region. Two of these port cities—Philadelphia, Pennsylvania and Trenton, New Jersey—are located on the Delaware River.

As you recall from my last message, Admiral, we flew from Boston in Massachusetts to the state of New York. New York is a large state, which stretches all the way from the Atlantic to what are called the Great Lakes. It has lots of green countryside and several large cities. But the place we most wanted to see in New York was the city with the same name. New York City is the most populated city in America and one of the most populated in the world.

The first thing we noticed about New York City is how many tall buildings it has. There are so many skyscrapers packed so closely together that when you walk between them, you can hardly see the sky itself.

New York is very, very crowded. Many people come to visit and to live in this famous city. Most of the time the sidewalks are packed with people and the streets are packed with cars. Everyone seems to be in a hurry.

A large wave of people came to live in New York City in the 1800s. These immigrants came from countries all around the world. Sometimes they came because they were looking for a better way of life. You see, Admiral, the United States is a country of immigrants. Since the country's beginning, people have come from all the continents of Earth to make their homes in America.

Usually, the first thing the immigrants saw when they sailed into New York Harbor was a

Tall skyscrapers crowd the island of Manhattan in this historic photograph of the Port of New York in 1923.

gigantic metal statue called the Statue of Liberty. This statue is in the shape of a woman holding up a torch. This statue is supposed to stand for the freedom that Americans enjoy. We took a ferry out to the statue and discovered that you can walk up inside it. By the time we got to the top of the 354 steps, we were worn out!

Things to Do in Manhattan

When people came to New York from all over Earth, they brought along the different kinds of food they ate back home. So in New York you can get almost any kind of Earth food imaginable. The crew enjoyed sampling all these different dishes. In the area called Chinatown, we ate several of the crispy snacks called egg rolls. In Little Italy, we picked up some sweet treats called cannoli. At a hot-dog stand, we had Polish sausages called kielbasa.

But there's more to do in New York than eat. Lots more! New York is full of cultural attractions—concert halls, theaters, and museums. Broadway is a street lined with famous theaters where you can watch musicals and plays.

I especially liked visiting the Metropolitan Museum of Art, where you can see some of the most famous art earthlings have ever made. Because she's so interested in plants and animals, Lieutenant Koola preferred the Museum of Natural History. She showed me the big skeletons of some extinct Earth animals called dinosaurs.

Of course, we also went to the library. We found the New York Public Library in an impressive building guarded by two stone lions. We spent some time there looking up facts about New York and the other states of the Mid-Atlantic region. We found out, for example, that the area has a climate pretty much like New England's. However, the summers are hotter and the winters aren't quite so cold.

We also found out that the states of New York, New Jersey, Pennsylvania, Delaware, and Maryland are among the most heavily populated states in the country. Their many large cities are centers of industry and government.

In fact, the headquarters of the national government is in a place called Washington. Washington is in the southern part of the region. We decided to make Washington our next stop.

Exploring the Capital

Washington is the only American city that is not in a state. Since it is the capital of the whole country, it cannot be part of any one state because that state would hold too much power. So the city is in its own district, the District of Columbia. That's why Washington is often referred to as *Washington, D.C.*

On the way to Washington, we flew over some of the other interesting cities in the area. In Pennsylvania, we flew over Philadelphia. In Maryland, we flew over Baltimore.

We also flew over a big body of water called the Chesapeake Bay, which was covered with hundreds of small fishing boats. We had read that wonderful seafood came from this bay. Chesapeake Bay is especially famous for its crabs, which are supposed to be sort of like lobsters, but smaller and rounder.

When we arrived in Washington we noticed the city has broad, straight avenues. There are a lot of grand buildings where the people who run the government work. Maybe the grandest building is the U.S. Capitol, with its big white dome. This is where the Congress comes up with America's laws. The Congress is made up of elected lawmakers from every state.

To the west of the Capitol is a long grassy field called the Mall. Usually, when Americans talk about a mall, they mean a shopping center full of stores. But this Mall is definitely not a shopping center! Instead, it is a place where Americans gather for different kinds of big celebrations.

Right in the middle of the Mall is a huge stone obelisk more than five hundred feet tall. An obelisk is a four-sided shaft that tapers to a pyramid-like point. This one is called the Washington Monument. It was put up in honor of America's first President, George Washington.

At the far end of the Mall is the Lincoln Memorial, which honors another great American President, Abraham Lincoln. Inside is a big statue of Lincoln, three or four times the size of a real human being. He is seated in a chair, and looks very serious and commanding.

Near the Mall is the house where today's President lives. When we saw it, we thought he was lucky to live in the elegant white house with tall pillars in front of the door. Americans call the President's home the White House.

When it was time for some studying, we went to the Library of Congress. This is the biggest library in the United States. There, we looked up facts about the next region we'd be visiting—the South.

The Mall in Washington, D.C. is lined with famous attractions and historical buildings. The Capitol building, shown below, is located at one end of the Mall.

Exploring the South The South is a large region with a diverse geography, including mountains, rivers, valleys, and sandy beaches. The twelve states that make up the South are Virginia, North Carolina, South Carolina, Georgia, Florida, West Virginia, Kentucky, Tennessee, Alabama, Mississippi, Arkansas, and Louisiana.

The South Region

Two large bodies of water border this region, the Gulf of Mexico and the Atlantic Ocean.

The South is a big region of the United States. It includes all the states on the Atlantic coast south of Maryland: Virginia, North Carolina, South Carolina, Georgia, and Florida. It also includes the seven states of West Virginia, Kentucky, Tennessee, Alabama, Mississippi, Arkansas, and Louisiana.

The South has a different climate from the northern states we've been reporting on. Especially in the summer, it is much hotter and more humid. So on Southern farms, they grow different crops from the ones they grow on Northern farms.

In the 1800s, the two most important crops for Southern farmers were cotton and tobacco. These crops had to be picked by hand. This was terribly hard work, which most people didn't want to do. So the Southern planters had people brought over from Africa to work the farms. But the people who came over didn't come willingly. They were kidnapped from their homes and were enslaved. Then they were sold to the people who owned the **plantations**.

In the Northern states, many people disapproved of slavery. For this and other reasons, there was conflict between the North and the South. Then, in 1861, eleven of the Southern states broke away from the United States and declared that they were now a different country. They called themselves the Confederate States of America.

For the next four years, a bloody war was fought between the North and the South. This Civil War ended with the defeat of the South. The Southern states came back into the Union, and the slaves were freed. When we learned that Abraham Lincoln was President during the Civil War, we understood why his statue in Washington had such a sad, serious expression.

The Shenandoah River twists its way through the Shenandoah Valley in Virginia's Blue Ridge Mountains.

Most of today's African Americans are descended from the enslaved people who worked on Southern plantations. Since the late 1800s, African Americans have moved all over the United States. But many still live in the South. You can see the African-American influence everywhere in Southern culture, especially in the food and music.

The South is a region of great geographic diversity. We flew south and west to a mountainous area shared by the states of West Virginia, Virginia, and North Carolina. The scenery here is very wild. The mountains are part of the great Appalachian chain, which reaches all the way up into New England.

In the South the Appalachians are known by different names. In Virginia they are called the Blue Ridge Mountains, and in North Carolina, the Great Smoky Mountains.

vocabulary

plantation a big farm where cotton and/or tobacco were grown

We landed our ship in a place the map called the Great Smoky Mountains National Park. After landing we found a man wearing an odd round hat. He explained that he was a park official, or ranger. He told us that a national park was a place the government had set aside so that people could come and enjoy nature. This was only one of dozens of national parks, he explained. We asked why the mountains here were called Smoky. The ranger explained that sometimes the mountains seemed to be smoking because of the fog on their tops. We spent several peaceful hours walking through the woods that cover the hills.

Enjoying the Southern Coast

Next we flew back east, to the coast. The coast of Virginia, North Carolina, and South Carolina is covered with sandy beaches. We enjoyed walking in the fresh sea-air and observing the behavior of the people on the beach.

The most famous beaches on the East Coast are farther south, in the state of Florida. This state is a long peninsula. It juts out between two bodies of water—the Atlantic Ocean on the east side and the Gulf of Mexico on the west side. One of the reasons why people go to the beaches in Florida and the other Southern states is that the water is warm enough to swim in. The water is warm partly because of a stream of warm water that flows through the Gulf of Mexico and up the East Coast. It is called the Gulf Stream.

Florida is even warmer than the rest of the South. In fact, it stays warm all year round in parts of Florida. Because of the warm weather, farmers in Florida can grow fruits that can't be grown in the North, such as oranges. Most of America's oranges are grown in Florida.

After visiting an orange farm, we flew on to Florida's most famous city, Miami. Many people come to Miami to visit the beaches nearby. But it is also a big modern city, with a diverse population. We found that Miami was full of immigrants from Cuba and other islands in the Caribbean Sea. The Caribbean is the sea off Florida's southern coast. On the streets of Miami, lots of people spoke Spanish, the language of Cuba.

After leaving Florida, we headed north again, to visit the states of Kentucky, Tennessee, and Arkansas. In Kentucky, we visited a farm where horses are raised to run in races. The most famous horse race in America is called the Kentucky Derby.

In Tennessee, we stopped off in Nashville and Memphis, two cities famous for music. In Nashville, we went to see musicians play what's called country music. In Memphis, we heard an African-American form of music called the blues.

The Deep South

Heading south again, we visited a peach farm in Georgia. We also cruised above Georgia's capital city, Atlanta. Atlanta was burned down in the Civil War and then rebuilt. Today, it is the most important business center in the South. Georgia, Alabama, and Mississippi are part of what some people call the Deep South. When exploring this area, we found that life seemed to move at as slower pace than in the rest of America.

The last Southern city we visited was New Orleans, in the state of Louisiana. We especially liked the part of town called the French Quarter, which is full of old houses. Pretty little fences made of black iron surround the houses, and their balconies were covered with potted flowers. Just like Memphis and Nashville, New Orleans is famous for music, especially jazz, another kind of music invented by African Americans. When you walk around, so much music is coming out of the buildings it makes you want to dance in the streets. In fact, New Orleans is known for a once-a-year party when people *do* dance in the streets. It is called Mardi Gras.

New Orleans is located on the biggest river in the United States, the Mississippi. This broad brown river runs all the way down from the state of Minnesota in the northern United States. It is the most important river in the whole country for transporting goods by boat.

5 The Midwest

Exploring the Midwest This region includes eight states—Ohio, Michigan, Indiana, Illinois, Wisconsin, Minnesota, Iowa, and Missouri. Rivers and lakes are major features of this region.

The Midwest Region

Three mighty rivers cut through the Midwest region. They are the Mississippi River, the Missouri River, and the Ohio River.

Hundreds of miles north of New Orleans we came to another large city on the banks of the Mississippi River. The map said it was St. Louis, in the state of Missouri. Missouri is in the area in which Americans call the Midwest. Also part of this region are the states to the north and east—Ohio, Michigan, Indiana, Illinois, Wisconsin, Minnesota, and Iowa.

We stopped for a while in St. Louis. There, we took a ride on the river in a big white wooden boat with a couple of smokestacks. The boat was built to look just like a paddlewheeler, one of the boats that used to travel up and down the Mississippi in the 1800s.

The most interesting thing we saw from the paddlewheeler was a huge shiny arch of steel standing on the riverbank. The guide on the boat called this the Gateway Arch. She said that it was the tallest monument in the United States—even taller than the Washington Monument.

Reading about the Midwest in the library, we found out that the area has always been very important for agriculture. In Iowa and Illinois, we saw many farms where they grow crops like corn and soybeans.

The cornfields were an especially impressive sight, with their thousands of tall green stalks laid out in neat rows. Later, we found out that most of the corn is actually not used as food for people. Instead it is used to feed animals, like hogs, which are raised for their meat.

Midwestern farmers raise animals for other things, too. North of Iowa and Illinois is the state of Wisconsin, which is called America's Dairyland. It seems as if everywhere you go in Wisconsin you see cows. We heard that there are as many cows as there are people in this state. These dairy cows are raised for their milk, which is one of the favorite drinks of Americans. The

Cargo ships move through ice on Lake Superior, near Duluth, Minnesota. Large Coast Guard ships help break the ice so the cargo ships can deliver iron ore to a steel mill.

milk is also turned into other foods—like cheese and butter.

But don't think that the Midwest is all cornfields and dairy farms, Admiral. It also has a number of big cities that are centers of commerce and industry. Cleveland, Ohio, and Milwaukee, Wisconsin, are important manufacturing cities. Detroit, Michigan, is the headquarters of the automobile industry. In fact, one nickname for Detroit is Motor City.

Cleveland and Detroit are located on the shores of the huge bodies of water that are called the Great Lakes. There are five of these lakes: Lake Superior, Lake Michigan, Lake Huron, Lake Erie, and Lake Ontario. Rivers connect the lakes to the Atlantic Ocean, so goods from the Midwest can be shipped all over the world. But the most amazing thing about the Great Lakes, Admiral, is their size. They weren't kidding when they called them great. When we flew over them, they just went on and on—more like seas, really, than lakes. We measured Lake Superior on the map and saw that it was more than 350 miles long. Later, we read that it is the largest freshwater lake on Earth.

Visiting the Windy City

Chicago, Illinois, is located on the southern shore of Lake Michigan. It is the biggest city in the Midwest. Chicago is a center of transportation, where railways from both sides of the United States come together. It is also one of the major port cities in the United States.

Chicago is the third most populated city in the United States. Los Angeles, in California, is number two, and New York, as I said before, is number one. When we went there, Chicago kind of reminded us of New York. It is a big, crowded city full of skyscrapers. In fact, we learned that the first skyscrapers in America were built in Chicago, back in the late 1800s.

Today, Chicago has the tallest skyscraper in the country. It is called the Sears Tower. We rode an elevator up to the top. Since the tower is almost 1,500 feet tall, we were glad we didn't have to walk up, as we did at the Statue of Liberty. When we got to the top, the view was inspiring.

We looked down on the huge lake, blue and sparkling in the sun.

Later we walked along the shore of the lake. Wind from the water whipped against us, making us chilly even though the sun was shining. We had heard that Chicago was called the Windy City, and now we knew why. Or so we thought. Later, studying in the public library, we found out the *real* reason for the city's nickname.

Long ago a newspaper writer from New York called Chicago the Windy City. He did so because he believed the people there were always boasting about how great their city was. You see, Admiral, when Americans think someone talks too much they call him or her a windbag.

We didn't notice people from Chicago boasting any more than other Americans. But they did seem very proud of their city. For one thing, they're always talking about their sports teams. You see, Admiral, in America the big cities play against each other in sports. Three main sports in America are baseball, basketball, and football. In Chicago, we went to an old stadium called Wrigley Field to watch a game of baseball. We enjoyed eating hot dogs, drinking sodas, and yelling along with the crowd.

When we left Chicago, we flew over the northern parts of Michigan, Wisconsin, and Minnesota. The land was covered with forests. Not many people live in this area. Lieutenant Koola had been reading about the animals of the region. She told us about the animal called the wolf, a kind of wild dog, which used to live in many parts of the United States. But over the years hunters have killed so many wolves that now northern Minnesota is one of the very few places where wolves still live. Lieutenant Koola said that if we looked closely into the forests, we might also see moose and bears. We had no such luck. But, we were still in good spirits on our way to the next region—the Great Plains.

Wrigley Field in Chicago, Illinois, looks much the same today as it did in 1939, as seen in this historic postcard.

Exploring the Great Plains This region is located near the center of the United States. It includes five states—North Dakota, South Dakota, Nebraska, Kansas, and Oklahoma.

The states of Oklahoma, Kansas, Nebraska, South Dakota, and North Dakota make up the region known as the Great Plains. As you know, Admiral, a plain is a flat area without hills or mountains. Flying over it, we were amazed at just how flat most of this region is. We noticed, too, that there aren't as many big cities here as there are in the East or the Midwest. Instead, the land is covered with farms and ranches.

A major characteristic of the Great Plains region is the flatness of the land.

Flying over the eastern part of the Great Plains, we saw huge fields of wheat. So much wheat is grown in this area that it is called America's Breadbasket. In the western part of the region, we saw big cattle farms, where much of the country's beef is raised. Another important product of the region is oil. Oil is turned into gasoline to run the millions of cars that Americans drive.

Early Life on the Great Plains

When we read about the history of the Great Plains, we learned how much the region has changed in the last 200 years. We learned that if we had flown over the plains in the early 1800s, we would have seen thousands of animals called bison. The Native Americans who lived in the region hunted the bison for food. Native Americans—also called Indians—are the people who have lived in America since long before the European settlers arrived.

In the 1800s, European settlers began moving into the Great Plains, taking over land that had belonged to the Native Americans. They also hunted the bison, and they killed so many that soon the great herds had almost vanished. The Native Americans fought the settlers who were taking their land and killing off the bison. Then, troops from the U.S. army came west to support the settlers. After years of fighting, the army defeated the Native

Americans, who were forced to move to special areas called reservations. Although defeated, the Native American culture survived. Today, many Native Americans still live in Oklahoma.

People have always had to be tough to survive on the Great Plains. The region has little water and a harsh climate, with fiery summers and freezing winters.

In the Great Plains spring is tornado season. A tornado is a special kind of very destructive storm. Most of the tornadoes on Earth happen in a part of the Great Plains called Tornado Alley. Tornadoes are clouds that funnel down to the ground at winds more than 100 miles an hour.

In the northern part of the region, the winter weather is especially harsh. This might be a reason why the states of North and South Dakota have so few people. North Dakota is bigger than the state of New York, but New York has more than 20 times as many people.

In South Dakota, we visited an area called the Badlands. There we saw colored hills of rock carved into different shapes by erosion. Early Americans called this land bad because it was dry and barren.

In a national park near the Badlands, four gigantic faces stare down from the side of a hill. The sculpture is called Mount Rushmore and it is of four American Presidents: George Washington, Thomas Jefferson, Theodore Roosevelt, and Abraham Lincoln. Each face is almost 60 feet tall. As we flew on to the next region, the image of these men stayed with us for a long time.

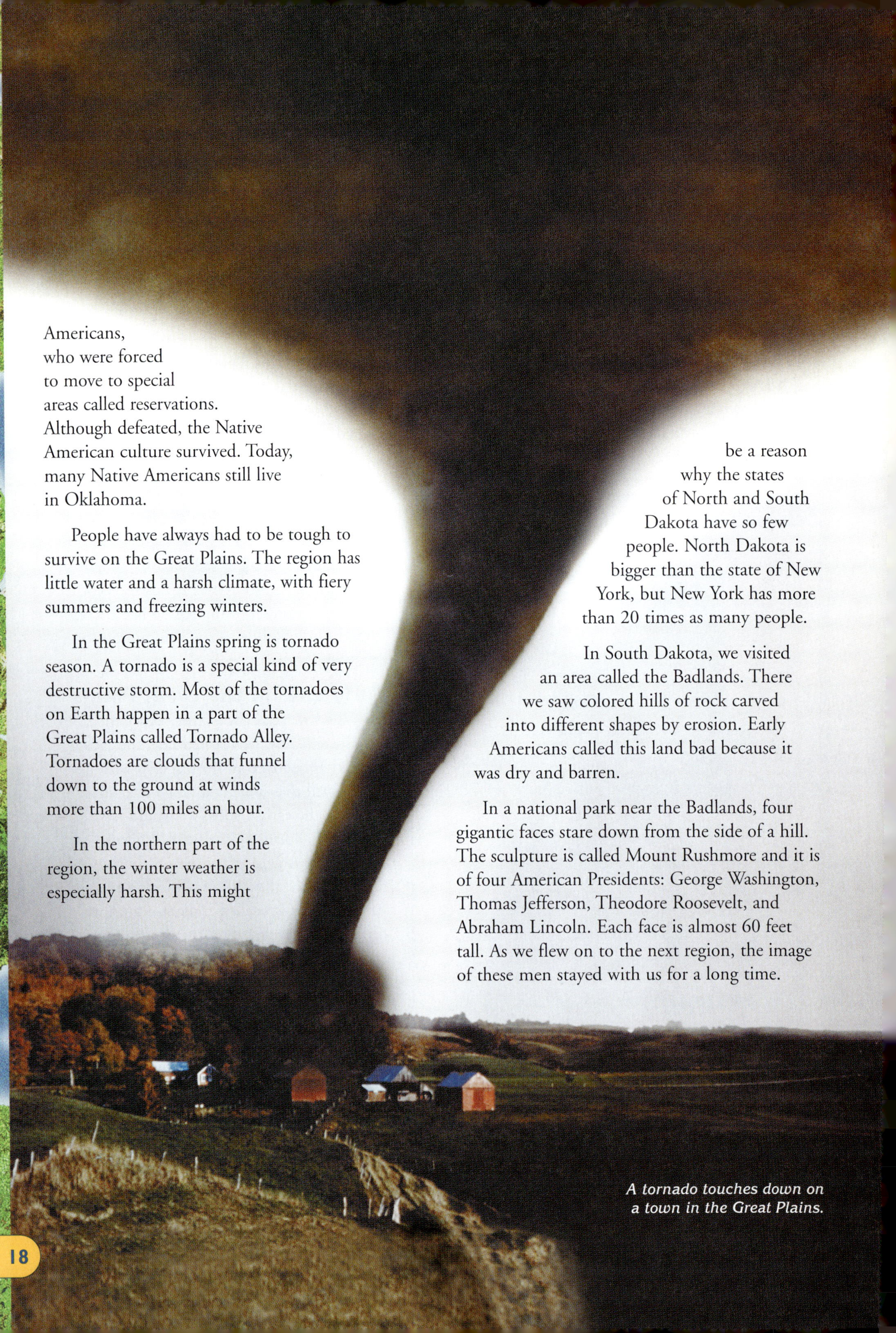

A tornado touches down on a town in the Great Plains.

The Rocky Mountain Region 7

Exploring the Rocky Mountain Region The Rocky Mountains form a long range that runs through all of the states in this region. These five states are Colorado, Wyoming, Montana, Idaho, and Utah.

The Rocky Mountain Region

The Continental Divide runs through the center of this region. It is a line of mountain ridges that separates rivers that flow eastward, like the Missouri River, from those that flow westward, like the Snake River.

Flying west from the Great Plains, we were greeted by a dramatic sight—a huge wall of tall mountains, stretching from north to south. Our map told us that this was the great range called the Rocky Mountains, which runs from Canada to New Mexico, and through the states of Colorado, Wyoming, Montana, Idaho, and Utah.

We noticed right away how different these mountains were from the ones in the Appalachians, the big mountain range in the eastern United States. Most mountains in the Appalachians have gentle slopes and rounded tops covered with trees. Mountains in the Rockies are more likely to have steep, craggy sides and jagged, rocky tops. Noticing how many of the mountains had snow on their peaks, we guessed that the Rockies were much taller than the Appalachians, too. It turns out we were right. The tallest mountain in the Appalachian range is only around 6,000 feet high. But the Rockies have dozens of peaks towering more than 14,000 feet.

Rocky Mountain National Park, in Colorado, contains many peaks over 10,000 feet high. Longs Peak, shown here, is over 14,000 feet high.

After the flatness of the Great Plains, we were eager to explore this mountainous region. Our map showed that Colorado had more and taller mountains than any other Rocky Mountain state, so we headed there first. We landed our ship in a park in the city of Denver, which the map said was Colorado's capital. We found out that it was a big modern city, the largest in the whole Rocky Mountain region. It is called the Mile-High City because of its high altitude, or height.

As usual, we went to the public library to find out some facts about the region. I wondered what made people settle in the Rockies during the 1800s. After all, most of the land in the mountains was too steep to farm. I found out that the early settlers mostly came to mine valuable metals that were discovered in the mountains. Among the metals they mined were copper, lead, and the most valuable of all, gold and silver.

Today, people who live in the Rockies work in many different kinds of business and industry. One of the most important industries is tourism. People come from all over the country to admire the beauty of the mountains and to visit its famous national parks. People also come to ski.

Skiing is a kind of sport practiced in many places in the Rockies. People go up to the snowy mountaintops. There, they strap long boards on their feet and slide downhill over the snow.

A Day at Yellowstone

From Colorado we flew north to Wyoming. This is the state with the fewest people in the whole United States. We flew over lots of wild, empty country on our way to Yellowstone National Park. Yellowstone is the oldest national park in the world.

In the day we spent wandering the park, we saw more amazing animals than we had in our whole time in the United States. Lieutenant Koola showed us big birds called eagles soaring in the sky. She told us that because it was supposed to be proud and free, the bald eagle was the national symbol of the United States.

Then she pointed out a herd of shaggy animals with horns and humped backs. "Remember the bison we read about when we studied the Great Plains?" she said. "That's what those animals are. They were almost killed off by hunters in the 1800s, but then the government decided to protect them in parks like this. Now there are thousands of them in Yellowstone."

In another field, Lieutenant Koola showed us some animals that looked like deer but were much bigger. On their heads were gigantic antlers, or horns, that branched out into many sharp points. Lieutenant Koola said that they were elk. Lieutenant Koola also told us about grizzly bears. "Grizzlies," she said, "usually stay hidden in the woods, but if they smell food, they come looking for it. People who camp overnight in Yellowstone hang their food from high tree branches so it won't attract the bears."

Brown bears, such as this one, can be found in Yellowstone National Park.

Later Lieutenant Koola took us to a place where a sign said Old Faithful. We wondered what Old Faithful was—another kind of animal, maybe? But there weren't any animals around. Lieutenant Koola said, "Just wait." Suddenly a huge jet of steaming water came bursting out of the ground and shot at least a hundred feet into the air! Lieutenant Koola said, "*That's* Old Faithful. It is the world's most famous **geyser**."

> **vocabulary**
> **geyser** a hot spring that ejects water and steam

We asked her what made the hot water shoot out of the ground like that. She explained that deep inside the earth there is a layer of hot liquid rock called magma. In a few places on Earth, like Yellowstone, the magma is especially close to the surface, and it heats the rocks just under the ground. When water from the ground seeps into the hot rocks, it boils and starts to turn into steam.

Pressure builds up, and the water and steam burst out of the ground together—and that is what's called a geyser. I said it sounded as if we were standing on top of a giant teakettle.

After leaving Wyoming, we flew north to Montana, another state with lots of magnificent scenery and very few people. In the northwestern part of the state we flew over mountains and valleys that had been carved out tens of thousands of years ago by glaciers—huge slow-moving rivers of ice.

Then we turned west and south and flew over the mountains of Idaho. I said to a crewmember, "Guess what Idaho is most famous for." He said, "I don't know—mountains, maybe?" I said, "No—potatoes!" I explained that Idaho grows more potatoes than any other state.

We flew further south, to the last of the Rocky Mountain states, Utah. I had read that most people living in this state belonged to a religious group called the Mormons. They had come here in the middle of the 1800s because their religious ideas were unpopular in the rest of the country. They wanted to practice their faith in peace. Today, Mormons live all over the United States. But the headquarters of their church is still in Salt Lake City, which is also the capital of the state.

Utah is only partly a mountainous state. West of Salt Lake City, the mountains end and the desert begins. But I think I'll wait until my next message to describe the American desert. I hear there's *lots* of desert to describe in the region we're heading to next—the Southwest.

8 The Southwest

Exploring the Southwest **This region is in the southwestern part of the United States. The four states that make up this region are Texas, New Mexico, Arizona, and Nevada.**

The Southwest Region

The Southwest is home to the Grand Canyon, one of the natural wonders of the world.

Our next job was to explore the southwestern states of Texas, New Mexico, Arizona, and Nevada. First, we had to backtrack a little, flying east to Texas. This is a huge state—the map showed that it was more than 700 miles wide. Later, we found out that Texas is the second largest state in size, after Alaska. It is also the second largest state in population, after California. We certainly saw a lot of really big things in Texas—big cities, big oilfields, and big ranches.

In fact, we found out that there's a ranch in Texas that's bigger than the whole state of Rhode Island!

Texas raises more cattle than any other state. The cowboy, a person who takes care of cattle, is a symbol of Texas. In the late 1800s, Texas cowboys used to drive large herds of cattle hundreds of miles to market in the northern states. It was hard, dangerous, adventurous work, so many people thought of cowboys as heroes. But over time the cattle business changed so that there was less need for cowboys. Today, there aren't as many cowboys in Texas. There are, however, many Texans that still dress like cowboys. They wear cowboy boots and a kind of tall cowboy hat they call a ten-gallon because it looks as if it could hold that much water.

Another symbol of Texas is the oil well. Texas produces more oil than any other state. Oil was first discovered near the city of Houston in the early 1900s.

Today, Houston is the biggest city in Texas. The American space program has one of its largest facilities in Houston. One man told us that *Houston* was the first word spoken on the moon. He explained that when an American became the first human to land on the moon in the 1960s, the first thing he did was radio back to Houston.

In our exploration of Texas and the other southwestern states, we heard people speaking Spanish, the same language we had heard spoken a lot in parts of Florida. When we studied the history of the Southwest, we understood this better. A couple of hundred years ago this region wasn't part of the United States at all. Instead, it was part of Mexico, the country just to the south of the United States, where people speak Spanish. But in the early 1800s, American settlers started moving into the region.

In the 1830s the American settlers in Texas broke away from Mexico. Then, in the 1840s, Texas joined the United States. At the same time, a big war broke out between Mexico and the United States. Mexico was defeated and forced to give up the land that became parts of Texas, New Mexico, Arizona, Nevada, Utah, Colorado, and California.

Mexican culture still has a heavy influence on this region. Lots of the cities here have Spanish names like San Antonio, El Paso, and Santa Fe. Today, the region is home to millions of Mexican Americans, many of whom speak Spanish as well as English. Mexican influence is especially strong in the state of New Mexico.

One of the best things about traveling in the Southwest is the wonderful Mexican food you can buy everywhere. Many Mexican dishes are

Modern-day cowboys drive cattle near the city of Dallas, Texas.

made with a kind of thin pancake called a tortilla. I especially liked the enchiladas—soft tortillas filled with meat or cheese and covered with a spicy sauce called salsa.

Much of the Southwest is desert—dry, sandy land with few trees. The desert begins in western Texas and covers much of New Mexico, Arizona, and Nevada. Very little rain falls in the desert. In the summer it gets hotter than any other part of the United States—temperatures of 115 or 120 degrees Fahrenheit aren't uncommon.

The desert gets so hot in the summer that it isn't safe to walk around in. Luckily, we were visiting in the winter, so we were able to put our ship down in southern Arizona and have a look. The desert was very different from most of the other landscapes we'd seen. We almost felt as if we were on another planet. Instead of trees, we saw cactuses—plants covered with sharp spines. Some of the cactuses were short and round. Others were very tall, with thick "arms" sticking upward from their trunks.

The Colorado River cuts through **Canyonlands National Park** *and continues to wind through the Grand Canyon.*

Suddenly we saw something strange—a little bird with long legs running quickly across the sand. We'd never seen a bird run before. Lieutenant Koola explained, "That's a roadrunner. He can fly, but he'd rather run." She went on to say, "You know, a lot of people think there's no life in the desert, but that's not true. Look—there's a jackrabbit." We saw a large brown rabbit hop out of a bush. Then I said, "Wow! I've found a little lobster." When we looked down, I saw something that did look like a tiny lobster, except that it had a long tail that curled over its body. Lieutenant Koola yelled, "Don't touch that! It is a scorpion. It has a poisonous sting in its tail, and if it stings you, you'll get very sick." When I heard that, I jumped back a couple of feet.

After we'd explored the desert for a little while, I decided that we should get back in our ship and fly to northern Arizona. There was a deep, wide hole in the ground that I wanted to see—the Grand Canyon. The Grand Canyon is one of the great natural wonders of America. It is a gigantic **gorge** carved out by the Colorado River, a mile deep and 18 miles across. If you peer over the edge, you can see the silver river glistening far, far down at the bottom. The walls of the canyon are all different colors—red, brown, white, and yellow. The colors vary because they are made of layers of different kinds of rock. Like most visitors to the canyon, we just stood there for a long time, looking at it in awe.

vocabulary
gorge a deep passage with steep rock sides

Exploring the West Coast **This region is made up of three states that border the Pacific Ocean. These states are Washington, Oregon, and California.**

After flying over Nevada, we headed west again toward the Pacific Ocean. The part of the United States that borders on the Pacific is known as the West Coast. There are three states on the West Coast—California, Oregon, and Washington. California is by far the biggest of the three, covering two-thirds of the coast. It also has more people than any other state.

The West Coast Region

A long chain of mountains, called the Coast Ranges, extends along the coast from northern Washington to southern California.

We decided to begin our exploration of California in Los Angeles, the biggest city in the state. Flying over the city, we were amazed by just how big it was. It spread out as far as the eye could see in every direction. We learned that big roads called freeways tie this sprawling city together. Los Angeles is so spread out that people sometimes spend hours every day in their cars, driving from home to work and back again. Since almost everyone has a car, there are too many cars on the roads, and traffic gets jammed. Americans call the times they drive to work in the morning and back home at night rush hour.

Los Angeles is home to people of many different backgrounds. For example, there are European Americans, Asian Americans, African Americans, and Hispanic Americans, to name a few. As you wander around L.A.—as the people who live there call it—you hear not only English and Spanish, but also languages such as Japanese and Korean.

Los Angeles is famous for its beautiful sandy beaches. On summer days the beaches are packed with people who have come there to enjoy themselves. We were there in the winter, so there weren't as many people on the beach. But we did get to see some people surfing. A surfer paddles out into the water with a long board. He waits for a big wave

The Hollywood sign sits high in the hills of Los Angeles, California.

to arrive. Then, he actually *stands up* on the board and glides down the wave—a little bit like the skiers we saw gliding down the snowy hillsides in Colorado.

Los Angeles is also famous for being the world capital of the movie business. As you know, Admiral, earthlings are very fond of sitting in pitch-black rooms and looking at the flickering pictures they call movies. The best-known actors and actresses who appear in these movies are called stars. Americans almost seem to worship them. In fact, I saw something very odd in a part of L.A. called Hollywood, where thousands of movies have been made. It was a place where movie stars had stuck their hands and feet in soft cement so that when the cement hardened, people could come to see their handprints and footprints.

Los Angeles is in the southern part of California. Flying north to explore the rest of the state, we saw some very different landscapes. To the north, the California coast becomes rocky rather than sandy. Tall cliffs plunge down to the ocean, and huge waves explode against the rocks.

Mountains, Valleys, and Steep Hills

Flying inland from the coast, we crossed a range of mountains. Then, we came to a long valley that stretches all the way down the center of the state. When we flew low over the valley, we saw that it was covered with farms. Later, we learned that this is one of the most important food-growing regions of the United States.

Flying further east, we came to a range of tall mountains, which the map calls the Sierra Nevada. According to the map, the tallest mountain in the range is Mount Whitney. Later, we learned that this is the tallest mountain in the United States outside of Alaska. As beautiful as the mountains were, we were eager to see California's other famous city, San Francisco. So we turned our ship back toward the coast. San Francisco is very different from Los Angeles. San Francisco is full of elegant new skyscrapers as well as lovely old houses. Its parks are lush and green, displaying interesting trees and flowers collected from all over Earth. The city sits beside a beautiful blue bay. Spanning the bay is the famous Golden Gate Bridge. The bridge's two towers are 70 stories tall, and they're connected to the bridge by great swooping cables.

Much of San Francisco is built on steep hills. At the end of each day's exploring, we were worn-out and aching from all that climbing up and down. We learned that over a hundred years ago, someone felt sorry for the horses that had to haul heavy wagons up the steep hills. He felt so sorry for them that he invented a new way to haul things in San Francisco. It was a kind of little train, called a cable car, which was pulled along by an iron rope set in the ground. Today, people come from all over the world to ride the cable cars up San Francisco's hills.

From the top of the 605-foot-high Space Needle, spectators can see a magnificent view of the city of Seattle.

After leaving San Francisco, we flew north to explore the states of Oregon and Washington, which make up the area called the Pacific Northwest. From the air we noticed a long mountain range which runs through both states from north to south. The map said that these were called the Cascade Mountains. Later we found out that these mountains were very important to the climate of the region.

When winds blow in from the Pacific, they pick up lots of moisture from the sea. When the air rises to cross the mountains, it cools off. Since cold air holds less moisture than warm air, the moisture falls as rain—*lots* of rain. The western part of Oregon and Washington is one of the rainiest areas in the United States.

We were amazed by how wet the area was—it drizzled almost the whole time we were there. But we were also surprised at how green it was. All that rain has helped give life to great forests full of towering trees. Lots of people in this region make their living by logging—cutting down trees to use for building or to make products like paper. But many of the trees are protected from cutting and set aside in national parks for people to enjoy.

After leaving the park we flew off to visit Seattle, Washington, which is the biggest city in the Pacific Northwest. Maybe because it rains so much, Seattle is full of coffeehouses. The most famous building in Seattle is known as the Space Needle. It is a tall tower with a funny-looking round top shaped sort of like the toy that Americans call the yo-yo. The tower is known as the Space Needle because the top is supposed to look like the sort of spaceship that aliens from another planet might use to visit Earth. Of course, it looks nothing like a real spaceship. We all had a good laugh over this. Earthlings can be so funny!

10 Alaska and Hawaii

Exploring Alaska and Hawaii **Alaska and Hawaii are states that border the Pacific Ocean. Alaska is the largest state in the United States. Hawaii is made up of a chain of 8 small islands and 124 even smaller islands. The most southern point of the United States is in Hawaii.**

Although Alaska is a part of the United States, it is closer to Russia and Canada than to the continental United States.

Well, Admiral, we've described our journeys through the 48 connected states of the United States. "Wait!" I hear you saying. "Didn't you say there were 50 states?" You're right, there are 50. But two of them, Alaska and Hawaii, aren't connected to the rest. Alaska is located 500 miles to the north of Washington State. To get there, you have to fly or drive across the country of Canada. Hawaii is located 2,000 miles west of California, in the middle of the Pacific Ocean. To get there, you have to fly or sail across the sea.

Alaska and Hawaii were the last two states to become part of the United States.

Sunrays reflect on the snow as a dogsled team runs in the Iditarod Race near Nome, Alaska. The Iditarod Race is an annual dogsled competition that covers 1,160 miles from Anchorage to Nome.

Alaska is the biggest American state by far. Two Texases could fit inside it. Yet few people, under a million, live in this vast space. Most of the people who do live there live in the biggest city, Anchorage. Much of the rest of the state is wild, rugged land—forests, rivers, lakes, and especially mountains. Boy, does Alaska have mountains. Seventeen of the 20 tallest mountains in the United States are located there, including the tallest of them all, Mount McKinley.

Alaska is so far north—just under Earth's North Pole—that it gets freezing cold in the winter. Temperatures often go down to 40 degrees below zero Fahrenheit. As we flew around, the mountains and glaciers of the state looked magnificent in their sparkling white robes of snow. Yet we wish we could have seen Alaska in the summer. Then, Lieutenant Koola tells us, the hills, forests, and streams are full of wildlife—such as moose, bears, beavers, otters, eagles, wolves, and mountain goats. She says that if you stand by the sea you can sometimes see a huge whale come to the surface.

The Islands of Hawaii

From Alaska, Hawaii was a long, long flight over the ocean. When we arrived, it was as if we were in another world. The state of Hawaii is made up of more than a hundred islands in the middle of the sea. Some of the islands are very small. Most people live on a few of the biggest islands. The islands are covered with forests, which are green even in the middle of winter. When we flew low to get a better look, we saw that the forests were full of brightly colored flowers. Then we saw something truly amazing—a red river of liquid fire running down the side of a mountain!

Lieutenant Koola explained that the mountain was a **volcano**, and that the liquid fire was lava. "Remember in Yellowstone, when I told you about the liquid rock called magma? Well, when a volcano erupts and the magma comes to the surface, it is called lava." Lieutenant Koola said that the whole Hawaiian chain of islands was formed long ago by erupting volcanoes. Some of them are still active, pouring out streams of lava.

> **vocabulary**
> **volcano** a mountain created by the eruption of lava from the earth

From there we flew off to the island called Oahu. We landed our ship in Honolulu, the biggest city of the islands. When we got out, we were amazed at how warm the air was. People were crowding onto the white sand beaches around the city. We noticed surfers in the water,

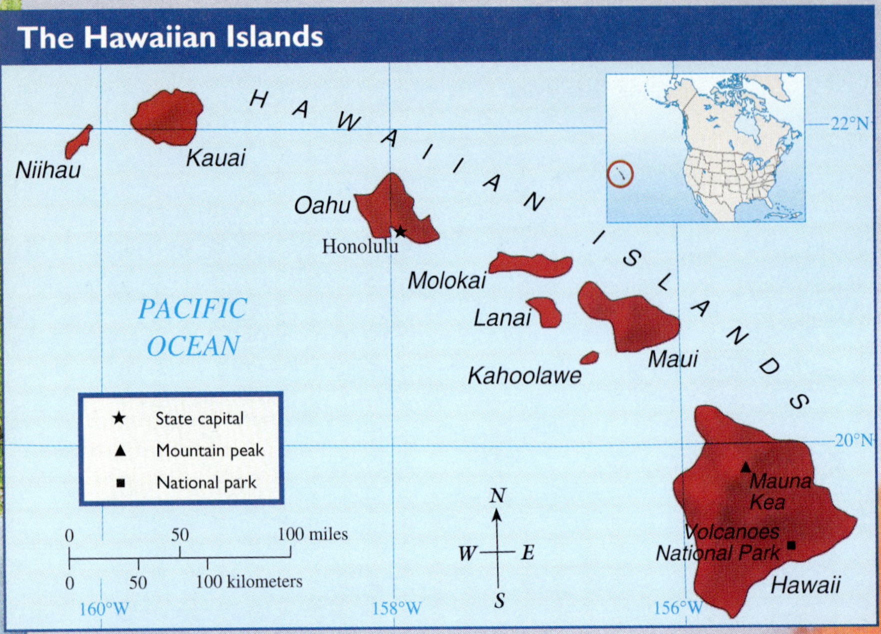

The state of Hawaii is a string of islands located in the Pacific Ocean.

and someone on the beach told us that surfing was invented in Hawaii.

In the library in Honolulu, we learned that Hawaii was first settled about a thousand years ago by people who came from islands further west in the Pacific. These first Hawaiians had their own culture, language, and religion.

Today, however, most people who live in Hawaii are Asian American or European American. Hawaii is the only state that has an Asian American majority. Only a small minority are native Hawaiians. Few people speak the Hawaiian language. But some old Hawaiian traditions are still alive.

One night we went to a traditional Hawaiian dinner called a luau. One of the things we ate there was a kind of

In 1986, and again in 1993, the volcano Kilauea *erupted in* Hawaii Volcanoes National Park*, creating lava flows as shown here.*

porridge called poi. You eat poi with your fingers. We also enjoyed the main dish, which was roast pork. The dessert was fresh pineapple. Most of America's pineapples come from Hawaii.

After dinner, we watched some Hawaiian women perform a traditional dance called the hula. Afterward, the dancers put chains of flowers around our necks. These flower-chains are called leis. They're given to visitors as a way of saying "welcome."

Hawaii was a friendly and beautiful place. But we knew that it was time to head home to Proteus. Right now, our ship is leaving Earth's atmosphere.

As I look back at the blue planet, I think of everything we've seen and learned in our year and a half of exploring. America, we learned, is big crowded cities and vast, empty deserts. It is towering mountains and deep canyons. It is forests and farmland, beaches and swamps. It is Hawaii's rivers of fire and Alaska's rivers of ice. The people of America are just as diverse as its landscape. They come from every corner of the earth, so that America has a culture that is made up of many different cultures.

I am still wearing the lei that the Hawaiian hula dancers gave me. It reminds me of something I learned from some people who spoke Hawaiian. They told me that there is one Hawaiian word that every visitor to the islands learns. It is *Aloha*. It means both "hello" and "goodbye." I like that. I think what it means is that saying hello and saying goodbye should give you the same happy feeling. After all, it is good to visit a new place, but it is also good to go home. If you liked the new place, there is always a chance you will visit it again.

I am signing off now, Admiral. I will see you soon. For now, I will just say: "Aloha, America! Aloha, Earth!"

Glossary

climate the pattern of weather in a place over a long period of time

geyser a hot spring that ejects water and steam

gorge a deep passage with steep rock sides

landform a feature of the earth's surface created by nature

plantation a big farm where cotton and/or tobacco were grown

port a place on a river, lake, or ocean where ships can safely unload and load supplies

region an area of land whose parts have one or more common characteristics

volcano a mountain created by the eruption of lava from the earth

CREDITS

All photographs © Pearson Learning unless otherwise noted.

PHOTOS:
Cover:
Pearson Learning.
Interior:
1: *t.r.* NASA; *b.r.* Photo Library International/Corbis. 5: *t.* Jeffrey L. Rotman/Corbis; *t.r.* Michael S. Yamashita/Corbis. 6: Craig Lovell/Corbis. 7: Francis G. Mayer/Corbis. 9: The Mariners Museum/Corbis. 10: Dean Conger/Corbis. 12: Richard A. Cook/Corbis. 15: James L. Amos/Corbis. 16: Lake County Museum/Corbis. 18: Jim Zuckerman/Corbis. 20: David Muench/Corbis. 21: Galen Rowell/Corbis. 23: Bettmann/Corbis. 24: David Muench/Corbis. 26: Douglas Sloan/Corbis. 27: Joel W. Rogers/Corbis. 29: Paul A. Saunders/Corbis. 30: Douglas Peebles/Corbis.

Maps:
2, 4, 8, 11, 14, 17, 19, 22, 25, 28, 30: Mapping Specialists, Ltd.

Border Art:
Joe LeMonnier.